Plant Secrets

Emily Goodman • Illustrated by **Phyllis Limbacher Tildes**

Charlesbridge

These are seeds.

PANSY
200 MG

PUMPKIN
BIG GUY
4.80 G
PRIZE-WINNER!

NASTURTIUM
7.50 G
New Annual

Some are big and round.

Some are as small as specks of dust.

Some have hard coats you can crack.

Some are black.

Some are brown.

Some are pinkish and some are striped.

But all these seeds have a SECRET.

**Hidden inside each seed
is a tiny new plant.**

Put the seeds in soil.
Give them water, and sun, and air.
If they get everything they need,
seeds can help their plants grow.

Here are seeds of rose, oak, pea, and tomato.
Can you tell which is which? Not yet?

Next come plants.

Some are taller than a person.
Some are shorter than a cat.
Some have green stems.
Others have wood.
Plants have different kinds of leaves.
Some are round, like plates.
Others are narrow, like needles.
Some are thick and rubbery.
Some are thin, like paper.

But all these plants have a SECRET.

Plants can grow flowers.

Give them soil, and sun, and water, and air.
If they get everything they need, plants
can make flowers.

Here are our four plants: rose, oak, pea, and tomato.
Can you tell which is which?

Next come flowers.

Some look like little suns.

Some look like balls of fuzz.

Some look like stars.

Others look like bells, or bowls, or feathers.

Some flowers have many petals.

Some have none.

They can be bright purple, or blue, or orange.

They can be pale colors, or brown.

But all these flowers have a SECRET.

Hidden inside each flower are parts that can make a fruit.

Give flowers sun, and soil, and water, and air.
Give them pollen from the right plant, carried
by wind or bee.
If they get everything they need, flowers
can grow into fruits.

Here are flowers of rose, oak, pea, and tomato.
Now can you tell which is which?

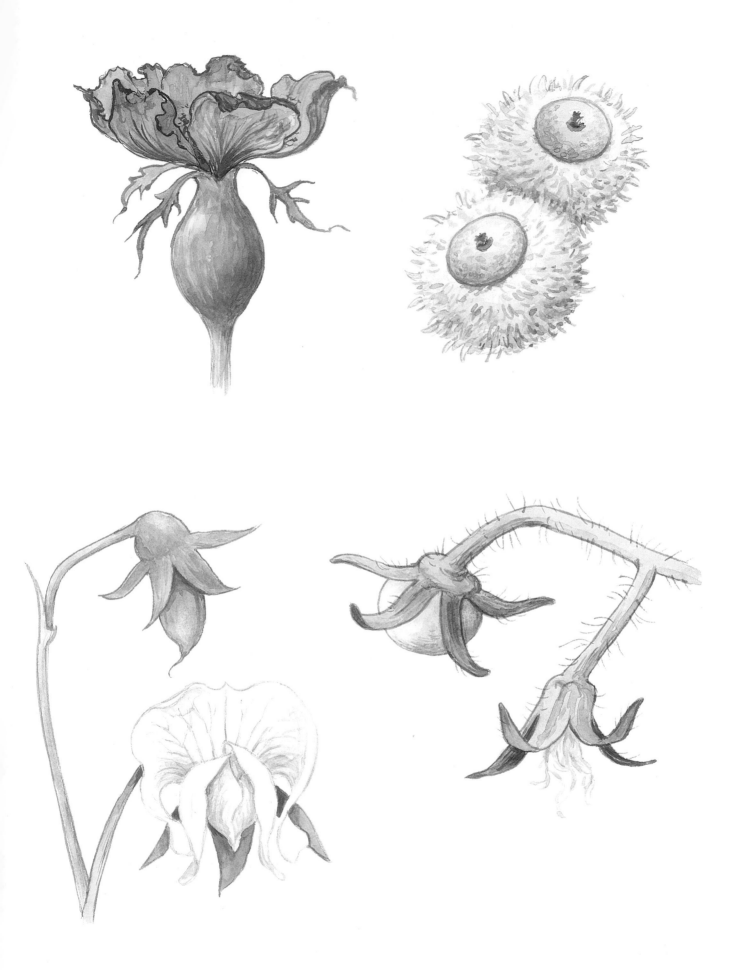

Next come fruits.

Some are red.

Some are green.

Some are brown and some are purple.

Some are good to eat—sweet and juicy.

Some are sour.

Some are not for eating at all.

Some are soft.

Some have a hard shell.

Some grow in clusters.

But all these fruits have a SECRET.
Can you guess what's inside?

Hidden inside fruits are . . .

rose

pea

SEEDS!

oak

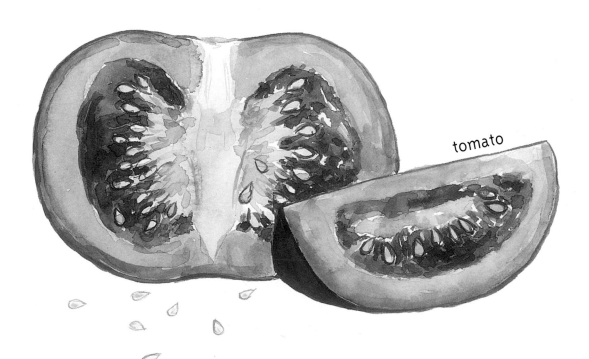

tomato

Plants have found many different ways to grow and reproduce. Most plants—like peas, oak trees, roses, and tomatoes—follow the stages described in this book: seed, plant, flower, and fruit.

Some stages are more important to people: the flower stage of roses, or the fruit stage of tomatoes. But all the stages are important to the plant.

SEED

A seed is a packet holding a young plant and food for the plant to use as it sprouts. We know peas best in their seed stage.

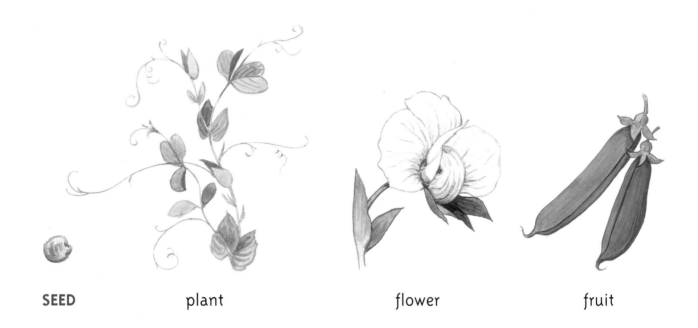

SEED   plant   flower   fruit

Peas

Peas are related to beans, wisteria vines, and redbud trees. All these plants have similar "pea flowers": upper and lower "lips" of petals around an open mouth. Peas are originally from Europe and the Middle East and have been eaten there since prehistoric times. Today they are planted all around the world. We usually eat the seed (the pea), but some kinds of peas are bred to make the fruit (the pod) tender and tasty. You can grow fresh peas indoors on a windowsill.

PLANT

Once it has sprouted, a plant can make its own food from sunlight. People and animals cannot do this. We know oak trees best in their plant stage.

seed   **PLANT**   flower   fruit

Oak trees

Oaks grow in many parts of the world. They are some of the largest trees in the forest and can live to be hundreds of years old. Many kinds of oak grow strong, hard trunks that can be used to make almost any wooden object people need: houses, furniture, wood floors, ships, wagons, barrels, or tools. Oak seeds, found inside the acorn (the fruit), are eaten by many kinds of animals: bears, deer, birds, ducks, and, of course, squirrels! Even people can eat certain kinds of acorns if they are made into flour for bread.

FLOWER

Flowers help the plant reproduce. When we think of a flower, we usually picture its petals. But other parts of the flower can grow into a fruit after the petals fall off. We know roses best in their flower stage.

seed   plant   **FLOWER**   fruit

Roses

Roses are part of a large family of plants that includes apples, cherries, almonds, peaches, and hawthorn trees. We usually grow roses for their beautiful flowers, and those kinds often don't form fruits. But other kinds of roses still produce fruits from flowers. These fruits, called rose hips, are usually red and look a little like small apples. Rose hips are high in vitamin C. They taste sour, so they're not good to eat by themselves, but people make jelly and tea from them. Birds, foxes, raccoons, and many other animals eat rose hips.

FRUIT

A fruit is a container for new seeds. Some containers are soft and good to eat. Animals eat them and drop the seeds on the ground. Other containers are hard. They protect the seeds through hot and cold weather until they're ready to grow. We know tomatoes best in their fruit stage.

seed   plant   flower   **FRUIT**

Tomatoes

Tomatoes are originally from South America, Central America, and Mexico. Tomato flowers and leaves look like those of deadly nightshade, a European plant with poisonous fruits. When explorers first brought tomatoes to Europe, people there were afraid to eat them because they thought tomato fruits might be poisonous, too. To scientists, tomatoes are fruits because they are the part of the plant that contains the seeds. But because tomatoes don't taste sweet, most people think of them as vegetables.

For my mother, who loves plants,
and for the GGs—our first fruit.
    —E. G.

For Lauralee and Amber with love
    —P. L. T.

Special thanks to Dr. Donald Pfister, Asa Gray Professor of
Systematic Botany and Curator of the Farlow Library and
Herbarium at Harvard University, for his expertise and advice.

Text copyright © 2009 by Emily Goodman
Illustrations copyright © 2009 by Phyllis Limbacher Tildes

Published by Charlesbridge
85 Main Street
Watertown, MA 02472
(617) 926-0329
www.charlesbridge.com

Library of Congress Cataloging-in-Publication Data
Goodman, Emily.
    Plant secrets / Emily Goodman ; illustrated by Phyllis Limbacher Tildes.
      p. cm.
    ISBN 978-1-58089-204-9 (reinforced for library use)
    ISBN 978-1-58089-205-6 (softcover)
1. Plants—Juvenile literature. I. Tildes, Phyllis Limbacher. II. Title.
QK49.G63 2008
580—dc22   2008007256

Printed in Singapore
(hc) 10 9 8 7 6 5 4 3 2 1
(sc) 10 9 8 7 6 5 4 3 2 1

Illustrations done in gouache on 4-ply Strathmore Bristol 500 paper
Display type and text type set in Triplex Serif and Triplex
Color separations by Chroma Graphics, Singapore
Printed and bound by Imago
Production supervision by Brian G. Walker
Designed by Diane M. Earley

pumpkin seeds

kidney bean seeds

apple seeds

sunflower

lemon

lime

grapes

summer squash

eggplant

wood sorrel

maple samara

cherries

chestnut
burr

blueberries

strawberries